Copyright © 2021 Blair F. Borders

All rights reserved. No part of this publication may be reproduced, distributed, or transmitted in any form or by any means, including photocopying, recording, or other electronic or mechanical methods, without the prior written permission of the publisher, except in the case of brief quotations embodied in critical reviews and certain other noncommercial uses permitted by copyright law. For permission requests, write to the publisher, addressed "Attention: Permissions Coordinator," at the address below.

Alpha Book Publisher
www.alphapublisher.com
ISBN: 978-1-954297-59-3

Ordering Information:
Quantity sales. Special discounts are available on quantity purchases by corporations, associations, and others. For details, contact the publisher at the address above.
Orders by U.S. trade bookstores and wholesalers. Visit www.alphapublisher.com/contact-us to learn more.

Printed in the United States of America

INTRODUCTION

The world is a noisy place—a cacophonous roar that assaults our ears, threatens our peace, and overshadows our inner voice. However, there is a wellspring of silence within that speaks in quiet whispers of wisdom.

For the last seven years, I have led an extremely quiet, contemplative existence. Reflecting upon this experience, the reasons for my prolonged solitude aren't important, only the lessons I have learned along the way. Although silence can be a harsh and unforgiving teacher—a lonely abyss—it has become my best friend, my ever-present companion through the vicissitudes of life. That silence unexpectedly birthed the contents of this book, a continuation of my work in *Gifts of the Dark Night*.

Blair F. Borders
West Palm Beach, Florida
May 18, 2021

ACKNOWLEDGMENTS

I'd like to thank my mother, Rosalind Borders, for her unconditional love and lifelong encouragement of my creative endeavors.

Original photography by Rosalind Borders and Blair F. Borders. Additional photography - Internet Public Domain

THE GRAVITY OF SILENCE

The Gravity of Silence

Beyond all religious, historical, and scientific understanding lies the mystery of consciousness—the greatest mystery of all.

The Gravity of Silence

The Gravity of Silence

To believe in the death of the soul is in itself bad science; to believe in the limit of its expression to only one lifetime, bad fiction.

The Gravity of Silence

<u>The Gravity of Silence</u>

Never fish for compliments; whatever you catch is sure to disappoint.

The Gravity of Silence

The Gravity of Silence

My heart is a secret symphony, a forgotten song in a world of smashed pianos hammering out discordant melodies.

The Gravity of Silence

The Gravity of Silence

Where words carelessly muddle, silence clearly reveals.

The Gravity of Silence

I believe in magic…the unparalleled beauty of the natural order is all the evidence I need.

<u>The Gravity of Silence</u>

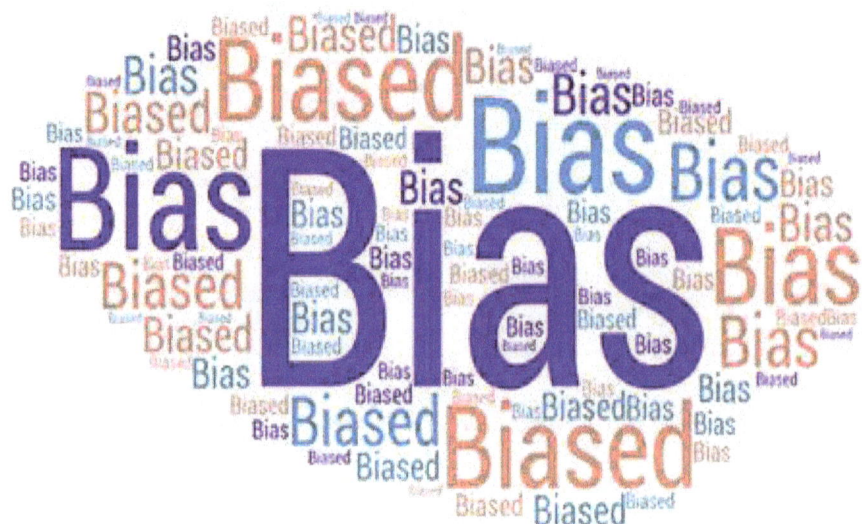

The Gravity of Silence

Ever notice how people who don't know what confirmation bias is seem to suffer from it most?

<u>The Gravity of Silence</u>

<u>The Gravity of Silence</u>

Don't confuse the personal with the autobiographical. People's comments, judgments, and observations about you may appear to be the former, when in fact they are actually the latter.

The Gravity of Silence

The Gravity of Silence

The ravages of time grant immunity to no one.

The Gravity of Silence

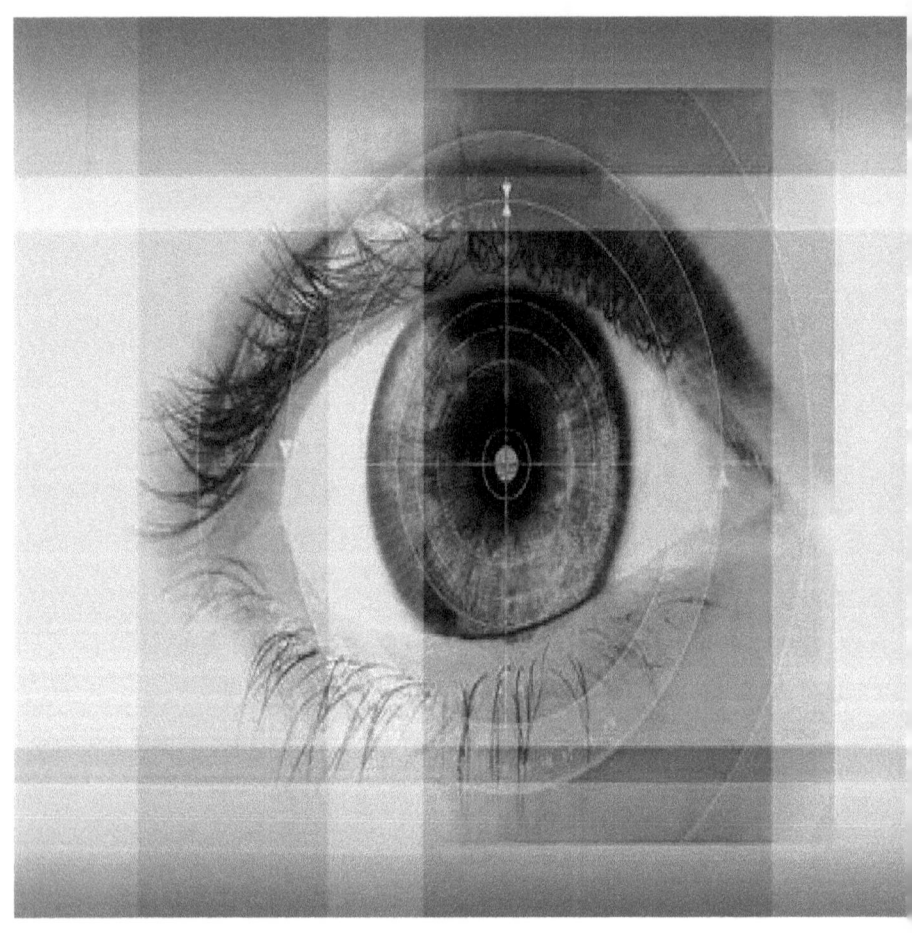

Spiritual truth doesn't depend upon your acknowledgement or approval for its existence; whereas, the quality of your existence depends entirely upon its acknowledgement and approval.

The Gravity of Silence

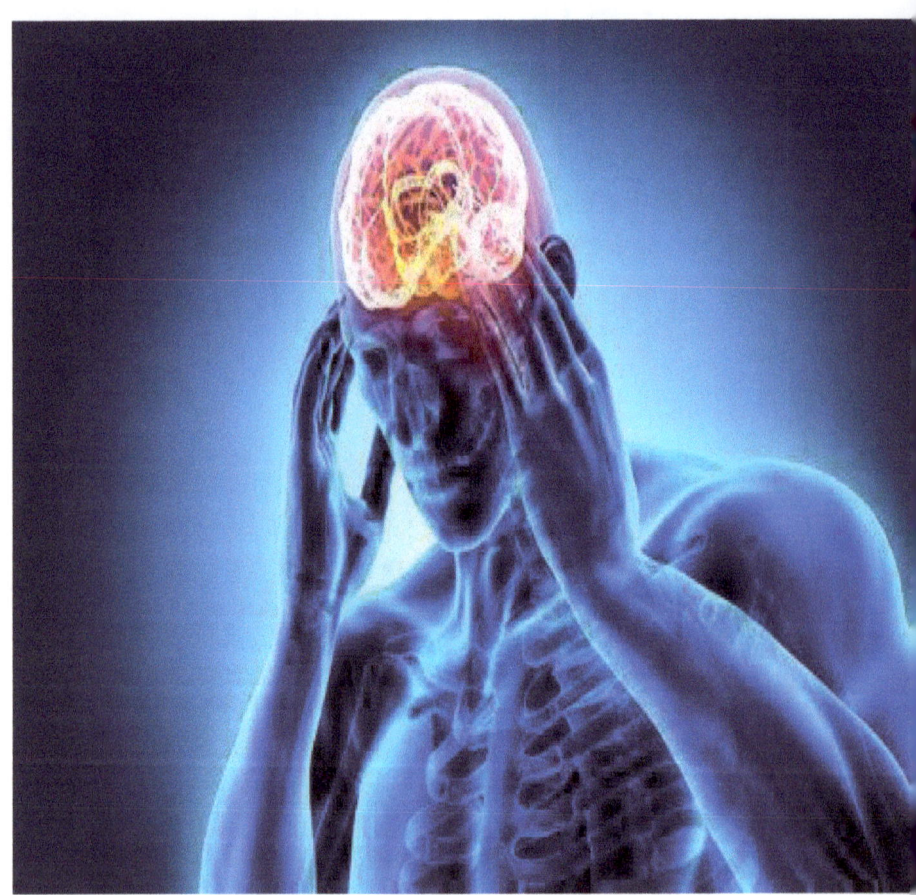

<u>The Gravity of Silence</u>

Technological progress is accelerating at a maddening pace, eclipsing sanity, reason, and, alarmingly—the wisdom necessary to sustain life on our precious planet.

The Gravity of Silence

The Gravity of Silence

Verbal communication not infused with healthy intervals of silence, and guided by wisdom, knowledge, and intuition becomes drivel—forgettable clamor in a world already strangled by noise.

The Gravity of Silence

The Gravity of Silence

Mind control is ubiquitous and operates according to the lowest common denominator—fear. Don't become a victim. Fight back by practicing the art of spiritual and intellectual discernment. Learn to distinguish between speculation and knowledge, image and substance, fantasy and reality.

The Gravity of Silence

The ship of every life eventually sails into unnavigable waters.

The Gravity of Silence

One stage of enlightenment unfolds when you develop the self-honesty necessary to stop judging others for doing exactly as you would have done in the same, or similar, situation.

The Gravity of Silence

There is a universal tendency for people to imagine the future while reliving the past, only to find that the future they imagined is exactly like the past they relived.

The Gravity of Silence

New Age thought popularized the belief in the law of attraction, taking it to materialistic and, in some cases, hedonistic extremes. Although an inherently valuable teaching which contains a core of metaphysical truth, it conveniently omits the darker shades of reality; that as simultaneously human/spiritual beings, our greatest growth frequently occurs as a result of experiences that are physically, emotionally, and psychologically difficult— even excruciating.

The Gravity of Silence

The Gravity of Silence

Poems, songs, and inspired writing are gifts from the ethers, transmitted silently to the quiet mind and creative heart attuned to receive them.

The Gravity of Silence

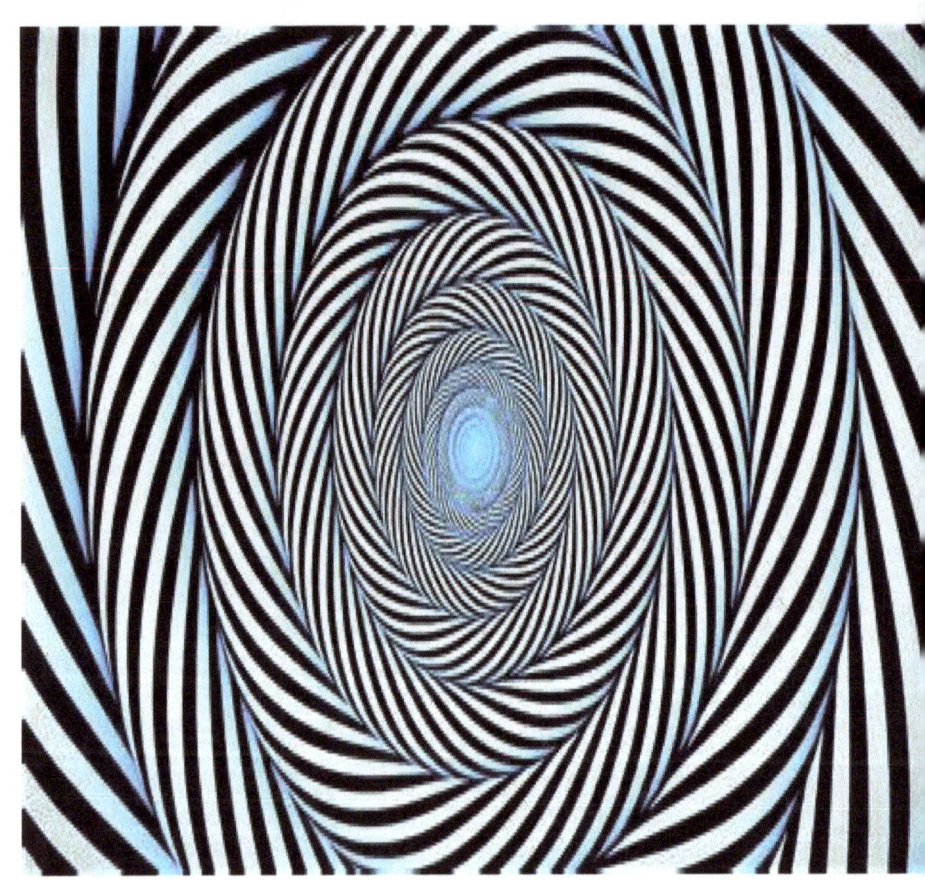

The Gravity of Silence

What many people call "truth" is merely a fragmented, subjective portal of perception.

The Gravity of Silence

Life invariably dismantles the illusion of personal — and even collective — control.

The Gravity of Silence

<u>The Gravity of Silence</u>

So much of our suffering is caused by seeking permanence and fixity in a realm of perpetual uncertainty.

The Gravity of Silence

<u>The Gravity of Silence</u>

If you hate the journey, the destination— no matter how glamorous— isn't worth it.

The Gravity of Silence

The Gravity of Silence

The degree to which you seek external approval is the degree to which you are held hostage by your own insecurity.

The Gravity of Silence

<u>The Gravity of Silence</u>

Modern civilization is so deep into digital bondage—so out of touch with the raw, organic pulse of life—that for millions, the beauty and majesty of nature are virtually non-existent.

The Gravity of Silence

<u>The Gravity of Silence</u>

There are essentially three kinds of people: those who fear intimacy more than they desire it, those who desire intimacy more than they fear it, and those who experience both in equal measure.

The Gravity of Silence

The world is a spiritual labyrinth masquerading as a physical jungle.

The Gravity of Silence

Reclaim your freedom; escape the pixelated horror of enslavement to supercomputers.

The Gravity of Silence

The Gravity of Silence

The etched grooves of negative thinking create the distorted record of wrong living.

The Gravity of Silence

<u>The Gravity of Silence</u>

Mass delusion flows like oxygen in a world where people fear fact, but love fiction.

The Gravity of Silence

<u>The Gravity of Silence</u>

Live not according to what you think you want, but instead according to what you know you need.

The Gravity of Silence

<u>The Gravity of Silence</u>

As intoxicating as fame may be to the ego, it is nothing compared to the simple pleasures and unmatched freedom of anonymity.

The Gravity of Silence

As a general rule, the more bombastic the ego, the more fractured and inadequate the actual self-concept.

The Gravity of Silence

The Gravity of Silence

The heavy static of excessive thought ruins the perfectly clear, beautiful broadcast called life.

The Gravity of Silence

The Gravity of Silence

The more you speak about something, the farther away you travel from experiencing its essence.

The Gravity of Silence

The Gravity of Silence

Conformity is a cage of flowers in a meadow teaming with life, a cloudless sky in a desert starving for rain.

The Gravity of Silence

No tempest
blows so
wicked
as a million
shackled
dreams—
the life
unlived, the
heart unseen.

The Gravity of Silence

The Gravity of Silence

In my soul there are oceans, rivers, deserts, forbidden forests where only the passionate and brave can enter.

The Gravity of Silence

The Gravity of Silence

If you fail to confront your fears, your fears will confront you—often at the most inopportune moments.

The Gravity of Silence

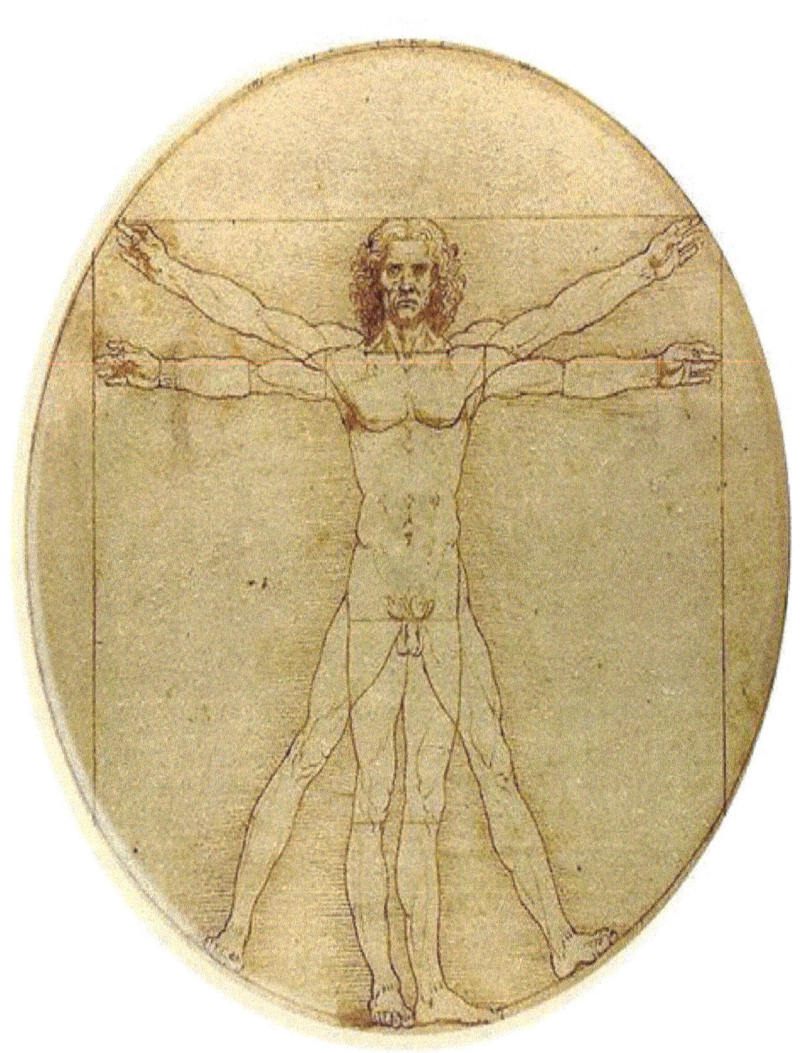

The Gravity of Silence

Human beings engineer their own subjective reality within an objective cosmic reality.

This complex interplay between dimensions is fascinating—both a masterpiece of art and a marvel of science.

The Gravity of Silence

The Gravity of Silence

The media-addled brain becomes incapable of independent thought, for it is controlled by forces designed to eliminate such a capacity.

The Gravity of Silence

The Gravity of Silence

Some things exist independently of your belief, whereas others exist exclusively because of your belief. The line between those two realities can be very fine…very fine indeed. It bends, blurs, and mystifies even the most inquiring and observant minds.

The Gravity of Silence

The Gravity of Silence

Humanity is caught in the grips of a tragic paradox. We now enjoy more channels of communication, yet suffer from less genuine connection than at any other time in history.

The Gravity of Silence

The Gravity of Silence

Covid-19 was, and still is, an unfortunate health risk—not a pandemic. The paralyzing climate of fear, economic devastation, and loss of freedom surrounding that fact represents the real pandemic. Now, after just eight terrible months, mass hysteria has transformed what began as the machination of Chinese scientists into the scourge of our planet.

The Gravity of Silence

The Gravity of Silence

For those who are unwilling or unable to think, feel, and believe for themselves, the straight-jacket of conformity eagerly awaits.

The Gravity of Silence

The Gravity of Silence

We are mystery incarnate—deeply spiritual, extraordinarily complex beings—reverberations of a cosmos spiraling onward toward evolutionary perfection.

The Gravity of Silence

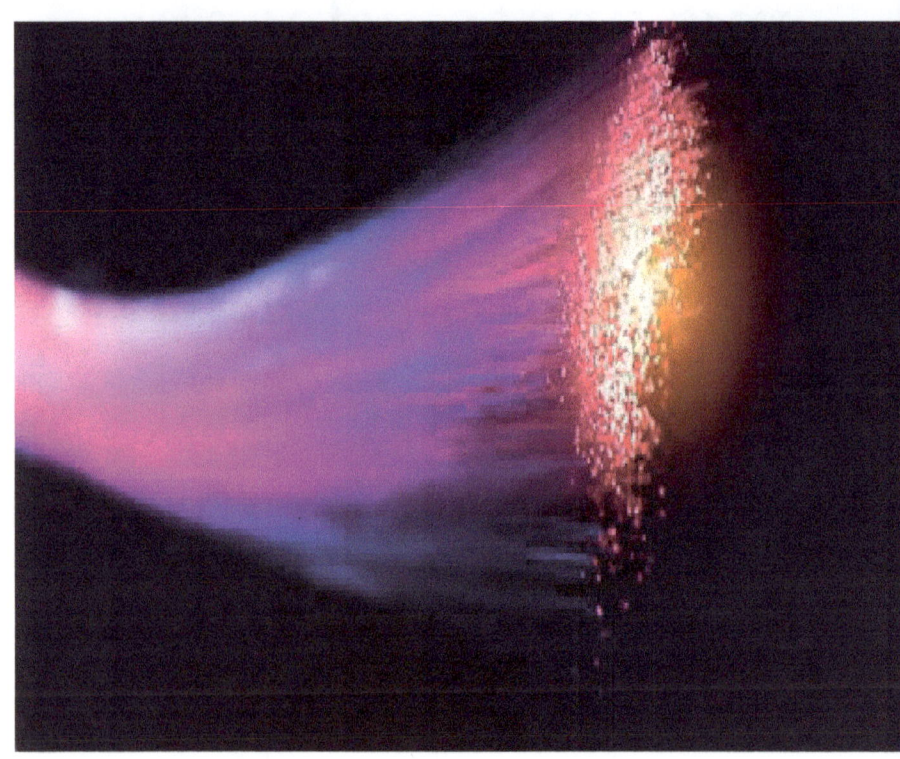

The Gravity of Silence

People don't need faster internet speeds, they need longer attention spans; they don't need more mobile apps, they need a higher quality of presence.

The Gravity of Silence

The Gravity of Silence

The profit motive, divorced from wisdom, becomes the deadliest cancer. Its purveyors level mountains, poison oceans, and slaughter forests—blind to their transgressions against natural laws and spiritual realities—never realizing that, with each hostile act, a part of them dies a quiet death.

The Gravity of Silence

The cruel mirage of purely mercenary endeavors becomes a haunting shadow that lingers in the desert of "success."

The Gravity of Silence

The Gravity of Silence

The Gravity of Silence

www.ingramcontent.com/pod-product-compliance
Lightning Source LLC
Chambersburg PA
CBHW050815090426
42736CB00021B/3462